loverboi.

ricardo bouyett

to my parents who sacrificed
so that I didn't have to
I thrive because of you
and hope you know that
all the compromises I make in my life
are done with the love and veracity
you've instilled in me

to my friends who lift me
when I'm too heavy
thank you, now it's your turn
to climb on my back.

to the love of my life
I am still here because of you

because of all of you

thank you.

contents

a humming surrounds my bedroom
the heat from the projector holds me
while the sweat running down my skin
begs to become the world's sixth ocean
but all I see are daisies.

come sit with me

Hi...I've been meaning to write to you.
I promise.
It's just one of those things where you check your messages
and then the bad news comes and the weather fucks up
and your lights turn off and it's 8 months down the road
and shit I forgot to respond.
But, hi...how are you?
Good?
Did you start a new line? I bet it looks incredible.
Coffee?
Well between my job and my projects and trying to find a new place to
live
I don't know.
Excuses right?
Let's make twenty of them to pretend
like it hasn't been 3 years since we've said,

"hello, how are you, I miss you."

Oh, these scars on my legs?
Don't worry, he can't hurt me anymore.

It sucked for a while yea, but I made it.

I sure as hell made it out of there...
out of there and back in again because fuck this
I'm so afraid of what's out there.
Between terrorists, racists, and rapists I don't know if I'm safe
or if he's safe or if she's safe or if you're sleeping better at night with
him.

Is it stupid?
To confuse the things I'm worried about
with this cringing nostalgia over something
that happened forever ago?
I don't mean to overuse you as my muse
but god you give me so much material to work with.

Or maybe it's all the other men that trickled in after you.

Hi...how's New York?
I like the snapchats you sent me
but why can't you sit down and talk to me?
Ask me some new questions I can't answer
with a digital copy of my naked body.

Did you get the roles you worked your hardest for?
Or are you still losing your phone on the subway?
Before you annoyed the shit out of me
I was afraid to sing again,
and before you taught me how to love again
I was afraid to make things with my hands that didn't remind me of
him, him, him.

But hi, how are you?
Get home safe?
Alright. I'll catch up with you later.

Maybe when we're good and old
we can come back to where we met,
and take a walk down to the lake.
Maybe, maybe you could come sit with me
and talk to me about
the movie theaters you fell in love with him in.

I'm all ears.

You can take my jacket if it's too cold,
don't worry about me,
my skin has cracked and
healed through so many tundras,
This.

This is nothing.

I dreamt once that the sun pierced
through my bedroom window
slid himself across my sheets
pulled them back gently
took his hands and caressed my cheek.
Waking me with a whisper, a tongue tied murmur,
"Please take my hands and follow me--follow me".
He pulled me out of my bed
and went straight for the window.
My arm slipped out of his grip,
the same trick time plays with our age.
He looked back, upset and confused.
I smiled an apology that stretched
between us and replied,

> "Oh, I would love to come away with you, but I can't.
> When you hold me close,
> when I'm with you, when I let you in,
> I burn and I am so tired of burning alive."

He tried to cry but he couldn't, he stood there
dug himself deep into my bedroom walls
took away the shelter I built out
of the promise I made my parents
and he jumped back into the sky.
I tried to cry but I couldn't.

i'm so fucking tired of love songs

My flesh flows into the ocean
Where he glides along the shore
Keeping company with the tide.
We're split inside the
moments burning at the hands
of sunbeams and clear skies
Planted in waves that stretch
Between bodies that haven't touched.

If I could construct my universe,
I would paint it with
the constellations that
connected me to him,

Him to me,
        Me to him,
                Him to me.

A fiction written with ink
made of hot and cold air
that when pressed onto paper
You master the weather
And can makeshift cities into the same
constellations you see at night.

If I could,
I would write
a thousand books,
where no matter
how crumpled the pages get
the ink of your name stays fresh.

Step into my fountain
look ahead at the channels
my water splits into.
Dumping out into streams, oceans,
and out of shower heads to soothe
your morning hangover.
I am as bountiful as the sea
and as wicked as the history
you wrote about me.
But still I love you.
I love you.
I just do.

God must have had a hard time letting you go
when she sent you to Earth.
You are divine,
I felt it the moment the doctor
pulled me out of you
delivering me from the universe you've created
into the one that created you.
I'm so grateful that you
are really here as I am here.
Life is a gift you've given me
a debt I'll never repay.
You brush my hair
look me in the eye before you hug me
And all you say is,

"it's okay"

It's okay to swim into the deep end of silence,
It's okay to hear the ocean calling my fevered name
It's okay to visit the attic in my mind and let the bats
fly out of my mouth to sing the opera where I wrote
all the things I hate about myself, the things that make
me lesser
it's okay to bow down to the universe
adore the reds, the blacks
of every forthcoming sky in the atmosphere
my lungs have nurtured.

It's okay to wave goodbye to myself in the mirror.
to say, "I don't know how to love you"
to be the whale that never comes up for air.
to feel the weight of all that I'm feeling.

She steps away from the hug
asks me a list of questions and comes
to the most important question I've ever been asked,

"Do you really think
my life,
your father's life,
your brothers' lives,
would be better
if you were dead?"

An ocean began to whirl behind her eyes
its sister swelled behind mine
I nodded my head "yes" and in the silence that followed
I understood what it felt like to feel someone else's
heart break inside my chest.

I brushed her hair out of her face
looked her in the eyes before I hugged her
and all I could say was,

"it's okay."

I'm shouting at the mirror,

"Am I too much, am I not enough?
Will he like what he sees,
will he butcher me in my sleep,
will he learn how to be nice to me?"

The mirror chuckles back at me
and I'm left there standing
Begging for the echo of the men
that buried themselves inside me to
feel my body
Feel it breathe,
contracting in and out
like the moon with the tide
expanding, receding

Pick at my skin like a dandelion weed,
see how lucky you'll be if
I love you, I love you not,
I love you, I love you not

I'm the appetizer at the chain-restaurant down the street
Ripped apart at the altar like bread and poured
across empty cups like wine
The shot you chase with a hint of lime,
generous in empty calories
full of I'm sorry's

I am shouting at the mirror,
I am shouting so many times
my voice reverberates off the walls
and pushes all the high school boys who
robbed me point blank of a chance
to know myself
out of the broken pipes in my throat

I look down at them
As I watch them gasp for air
The mirror calls out my name
And I look back at him
Only to see a
13-year old me
Smiling back at me..

I look at you
and I want to jump through
every different universe
so I can get to yours.
Knock on the door,
tell me I have all the right boarding passes.
You see your family fixed inside
my brown velvet eyes,
but when you met me in the atmosphere
you told me saints don't last long here.
You shut the door so fast my body caught splinters
and each one spelled out a reason to hate you.

But I don't.

You didn't give the monsters
inside of me a chance to say hello,
you summed me up after two weeks
of kissing me outside the drive-thru.
I felt more love come
from red traffic lights.
But I don't hate you.

I don't know how to.

I don't need you to love me,
I don't want you to.
I want you to fly out through that window
teach the birds living underneath the deck
how to stay quiet so I might sleep.

Little bird, little bird,
what's out there that's
making you sing so much?

Tell me how I've overspent my lips
on less deserving men.
I'm listening. I'm all ears.
Tell me how I've done it all wrong.
How I've surrendered myself
too many times too quickly.

I surrender, I surrender....I surrender.

I don't want to make a home out of you.
Not if it means changing the locks every night,
desperate and begging,

"kiss me, kiss me,
kiss me, kiss me,
'til I am reduced to nothing
but the gravity of a smile. "

I have no love for fuckboys
because I fucked these men over
and under my bed through the crevices
between my veins.
Fucking them physically, spiritually,
thinking I am closer to salvation by pumping blood
that carried their names to my heart.
These nights where when I knew what it meant
to be on the tips of tongues that refuse the whole of me
and outside on the street when it's pouring rain
I drop to my feet and I make-believe
I'm getting closer to finding the cure,
the secret to pulling my rapist outside of me forever.

These are
the hours I'll let you visit me:
7am to 3pm, Monday through Friday.
In the moments in between
I'll walk like a ghost
in love with a world
that didn't ask for me.
My forgiveness will fall
from my tongue
like honey spills from pot to cup,
a downpour of amens
slip from the guilt
stained on your bed
and you will stand there
wearing me like a crown
on your wedding day
wishing it had been you
instead.

My amen is sitting in the river
hold onto me love we're going for a swim
down in the city streets we'll find our namesake
the holy and the wicked, together singing
my amen is sitting in the river
link your arms with mine
hold on we're running down the stream
our children are waiting near the 'bend
singing songs of when we met
and all the times that you left
hoping I'd stick around with a light
guiding you back to our house
but I'm wet, drunk, and walking out
of the metra station, singing underneath
the tunnel echoes your name back to me
he's telling me,

    "baby I'm sorry but not sorry enough"

this couple walks past me
and tells me I sound beautiful
and I tell them,
my amen is sitting in the river

Raindrops fell from the leaves above me,
half-naked inside a torn up dress,
my body shook like thunder.
I was listening to the roars of the cars driving past
and I felt her.

I felt God within me.
No fear, no shame,
no hate could I spit at my reflection.
I was alive in this blessed storm
and I was gifted with the notion that
I too can be wet with glory.

I designed this kiss.
I wired it with pop songs
Hid it in the night so I could watch you
Look for me in nightclubs.
Sweaty, alive, and on fire.

I made you up inside the space between
The paper thin moths flying around me
I made you up because I wanted to be in love with
a version of myself
I could stand to live with
I made you up so I could destroy you
 without ending myself
I made you up inside the space
between these paper thin moths
so I could control my own mortality.

My manhood is a bible
Your tongue is the scripture.

My brain is a bedroom.
I moved in some new fake potted plants today
Because every now and then I forget to let the rain water soak me.
My bed sits on metal bars, holding me tight like my skeleton cages
my lungs.
Deep breath in,
Deep breath out.
My thoughts come in a 24-color box of crayons,
drawing memories inside stormy night car crashes.
I love it when lightning strikes and the crayons break.
My brain is a bedroom,
my heart is the tenant
And you are the guest.

I have to recite their names from memory
and spell their horrors with my tongue to the floor.
Every night my veins beg me to stay awake.
They would write love letters to my nerves
And my nerves would kiss me with the
fear I have met the end of me.
But the sun still rises, and I'm still
worshipping you on the floor.

I could read our story
By just one taste of your lips
Soft, sweet, poison
You held me baby
Over the edge of an ocean
That stretched farther than the Atlantic

Your stone heavy teeth
Keep me sewn into your bed seams.
I'm waiting for some sweet release,
But I'm finding that I need to be
Laying beside you right where
The ground ends.

inside a 35mm dream

We were driving in this big like almost SUV kind of car & we were on our way to some concerts & in between each concert we'd listen to our own playlist. I'd stick like half of my body out the window to feel the breeze or I'd be on the roof of the car acting a fool & taking pictures of everything. At all the concerts I'd convince people to give me money, I don't remember how but it worked. We made enough to continue our road trip & we hit up different hotels & stuff. I think we were heading to Portland or something, I don't really remember but I do know how much we both love the west coast.

We ended up in some big carnival fair type shit, it was hella colorful. Like the colors were really vibrant, lot of lens flares, like cool it JJ Abrams, this isn't your love story. We were at some of the games & you were playing this shooting game to win me a big ass pikachu & while u were playing I walked away & got on this Ferris wheel all by myself.

From the cart I was just looking at everything & everyone & I was just like sitting there, feeling everything. This part got really intense because I felt like I was inside that cart: wearing my jacket, feeling literally everything dream me was feeling. But anyway.

When my cart got to the spot all the way at the top it just stopped turning. I looked down & everything looked hella small but I wasn't scared which was weird since I'm genuinely afraid of heights. But I was calm, & the breeze felt really real and really nice. You won the pikachu & were wondering why I ditched you & you texted me "wtf" & I texted you back to look up & I was on the edge of the cart.

you & a bunch of other people were telling me not to do it. And I just kept repeating under my breath how everything's going to be okay. I felt really at peace. I take a couple steps back and I'm on the other edge of the cart & I turn around & jump so no one can see me fall and make impact. When everyone went to go look on the other side there was nothing on the ground. Kinda like I was never there, never jumped, nothing. Everyone left the venue & it was just you in the carnival holding this big ass pikachu wondering where I went.

He looked at me with a nervousness painted across his eyes

Me: "What happened?"

I'm caught between him wanting to smile and stay serious.

Him: "My life happened."

He's looking down at his food and he chuckles. Looks up at me.

Him: "But then I met you."

he smiles.

Me: "Man that must've been the worst thing that's ever happened to you."

he laughs.

happiness is swimming in the ocean,
walking back on the sand
to grab your towel to dry off
heading back to your
well air conditioned hotel room
to take a shower
and then letting
your tired ocean-kissed body
surrender to the cloud of comfort
that is the hotel bed while feeling
the absence of the sand
that touched your skin
and the waves that hugged you tight
all the while grinning slightly
as you fall asleep.

By the purple moon I find you
sleeping and dreaming about the world
and how it's better without you

darling, blues don't make us fools
following them turns us from one to two
baby listen I choose you

Truth be told I choose you.

Most nights the moon tucks itself
under the covers of my eyes.
It's too tired to command the
tides to wash you away
so it turns to me but all I know is red.
All I feel is red cast across my bed
so I let these feelings fuck me clean,
fuck me out of my mind.
So the moon can learn it
doesn't have to hide.

I lost my heart at the cinema.
I let it wander through the rows and the aisles,
and let it burrow a home in the moving images.
It was okay, maybe safer even,
to stay locked in the sequences
where sound is booming, yielding.

Not his alone, not mine alone,
but our heartbeats together drummed across
the vacant seats in the theater behind his eyes.
Like the projection kissing the silver screen,
I was his dreams, his nightmares.
We were stories woven into bodies,
recycling our histories until we made sense.
We always came back to the origin of it all
whenever we lost.
But now there's no starting point to go back to,
only an exit sign and
the waters ahead that
carry me gently to the next.

It's the great picture show
my heart is the director
you all are the crew
and what I choose to do
with the rain of humanity
is the ensemble, the story
the motion picture narrative
a century of memories
that spelled you out
under me

Do you think about kissing me
as often as I think about kissing you?
My body fits well under headlights,
steady cruising through the noisy traffic
between your lips and mine.
You don't love me, you don't have to,
just paint your grief all over me.
Lips first. Hearts last.
Can you find god hiding in the back of my throat?
She says keep on praying, pray your way through me.
Skin through skin, sweat beating out sweat,
break into me so you can get to yourself.

We have the same eyes, you and I
Because we are both exhausted.
But you wear yours differently.
You dress them up in rage and
There is no getting in between them.

Get in between me,
Take up your space within me.
Fill me to the brim so I can
Overflow and purge out the clutter of bodies
That stained my bed.

My sweat drops on my skin
like falling stars die across the sky,
and I carry a box full of questions that make you cry.
Because they remind you just how alone you are
and how lucky you'd be if you learned how to say yes
to love from your shaking hands.

Sunday morning came with
a deep red sky after he left me
it made Cupid jealous.
He thought I'd have nothing but rain
Falling at my feet yet here I am
giving birth to a bright new day.
Feed me your envy Cupid.
I want to taste disappointment
From the lips of someone
who finds love for everyone else
but not themselves.

What do you taste like?
Zinc? Lead? Water?
Let me teach you how
to put down your weapon,
let my kiss educate you
and instruct you on
how to give yourself everything
you give everyone else.

Feed me your envy.
It isn't serving you well.

I want that feeling.
I want to be in it, in control of it,
under the control of it.
Flirting with the boy who'll meet me
halfway at the altar.
My traumas and his in a basket
filled with flowers and fast food coupon clippings.
You may now kiss the;
I will love you until I am food for the trees.
You may now kiss the;
I will give my all for you.
You may now kiss the;
I will wait until the day I meet you.
Until the day my body meets justice
and your hands become
all the liberty I need.

Dead men slept where my heartbeat sang.
I picked them up with my shovel
tossed them into the air because
I've finally learned that my chest
is not a grave for aimless spirits.
I give you my limbs, my muscle,
my skin, my color, my lips, my teeth,
my eyes, my anger, my peace, my chaos, my all.
I give you my hand, pull me under.
Pull me out. Pull me back in.
I want god herself to cry at my funeral
because she doesn't get to keep my ghost.
I'll reach for you, tell you it's okay to love again.
It's okay to wake up to your reflection and
 shout "i love you" to a silent audience.

My little brother asked me

"Why do you want to die?"

I looked at him and an earthquake
couldn't even move my feet apart.
I looked at him and all I wanted to say was:

I'm tired of feeling everything all at once
or not at all and not being able to decide
when that may or may not be.
I'm tired of my rapist waking up inside of me
after I just put him down to sleep.
I'm tired of seeing everybody hurting everybody
and being blamed because I'm comfortable
crying in a fast food restaurant
instead of shoveling it all away inside
of alcohol, video games, and one night stands.
I'm tired of my skin breaking itself
so it can breathe for five fucking minutes
until the arms of every man who's ever harmed me
grips me and tightens to snap me in half
and the halves snap themselves in smaller halves
and every Wednesday morning I become
the dust you collect at the barbershop
when you sweep the floor.

I'm so fucking tired of existing
of being who I am, the guy who everyone says

                    "He's different".

What's so different about me?
That I feel? That I express?
That I dive into my deepest wounds
and somehow manage to pull out
a bouquet of flowers &
string out the letters for

                    "I love you".

That when you spin neglect,
indifference, and hate into
bullets inside my chest,
BANG! shots fired.

                  "I love you because I know
                      you're hurting too"

BANG! One round left.

                  "I love you because I know
                    what you're going through"

BANG! You thought I'd be
fucking dead.

But I'm not.
I'm still here,
and somehow that's "different".

I look at Gabe
and I don't say any of that.
I just look at him
brush it off
pull out these words from
the bouquet
that say,

                    "I'm just tired Gabe,
                        I'll be okay."

I am a kaleidoscope of emotion.
Every sliver of glass reflecting light
was born out of my holy mother's spit.
Weaved into a fine sheet lined in explosives.
I will stand in the middle of our backyard
and the sky will come down behind me like a backdrop.
My thoughts will detonate, screaming at each other,
screaming at the sky,

> "Give me love,
> give me more than my shoulders can carry!
> Crush me!
> I am ready."

I want to turn your midnights into tangerine skies
Breathe daisies into your empty garden
And watch the sky write love songs about us.

A little bit of you and a little bit of me
could give birth to heaven's envy
I want the flowers in my bedroom to rise
when I breathe in first morning's breath.
Blooming as my bones bend, break,
the muscles of my back twist too tight and loosen.
Surrender, surrender, I surrender to the wave of change.
To the ocean between my lungs
breathing your name in and out of orbit.
Vibrating in the strings of the night
I felt your lips tell me a story
that didn't end in lovers dying,
My youth ran down the river.
Wet and wild,
unscathed but beaten altogether.
The rocks begged to meet another dreamer
and the river granted them my skull.

I run around with this vendetta like a gentle giant
Hating you feels good for the night but when I wake up
I pray that you're doing fine.
My hips don't bend like they used to,
But your lips still taste like deceit.
We didn't hit much of the sky,
So stop acting like you're mine.
My love is a kaleidoscope
Made from my glass heart that
Bends and fractures light into
Physical love letters all stamped by your lips,
Addressed to me.

Late in the evening my wandering feet travel
back home to you.
To nothing.
To be met warmly by
the sound of dial tones and static.
There's not enough room in my body to store my lover's
crimes.
No jury, no verdict can guide me to what I want.
Love, everlasting.
As elusive as the breeze against my cheek.
Keep me in the company of ghosts.
I want to be held by the ether of their pasts
and the sustained by the promise of my future.

You'll look for me in other faces,
other voices, other lips.
Four months from now it will be
four in the morning.
You'll be sleeping with him
sweating out my name as he tells you
he loves you.
Four months from now
it'll be four in the morning,
your memory will spit out of me
at walls that hate your name.
To remove the stone from my teeth
you must kiss me gently.
Twice.
Toss me across the sheets
like confetti across a crowded room.
Illuminate the dark corners of my night
with digital lights pulsating with the names of men
I pushed out through my veins.
Tell me I'm pretty.
Decadent.
Monstrous,
like a night with a
blood red moon to hold.

Desire breathes into me like fire.
Reaching deep into me like a liar.
Men line up to ask me if there's room in my skin,
praying to their mothers that they find shelter
in between my no's and maybe's.
I'm overweight in pounds of empty beds,
crying out and calling for a truce between my body
and the doorman who let these men in.
Desire scars like fire.
I found salvation in between the crevices of their crooked skins,
following the lines on their palms
like a map to the holy grail.
I found salvation in craving
a fleeting taste of people who I know
will leave if asked.
Stars to skyscrapers,
we never really touch
but we're always close by.

I've drowned under the selfish waves of lovers before you.
My love, have you found patience inside of my bones?
I don't know how to feel your touch without
running through a minefield.
There are ghosts larger and scarier than you
that live inside me
and wake up when you kiss me.

Love, you are my last love.
If you're going to ruin me do it in a way that he hasn't already.
Your form of worship is torture and I am aimless,
guilty, too tired to tell you.
Can you see him laughing in my eyes?
Last love,
this is my last,
love.

I fell in love with the promise of healing.
With the promise of loving and being loved.
Discover in me what I still have not in you,
the wonder of love everlasting.
Build on top of the towers of your mind
the crucible of our youth.
Does he love me, does he not, would he date me,
could he wait for me?
Sing about it at four in the morning after I leave
and dive back into the waves of January strains.
Pass it along to the next ghost that meets
to kiss your stone heavy teeth.

The night whispered love songs to the morning.
She told her all the secrets she kept from the stars
and the morning lit up her fields with life.
I see love letters painted on every cement block in this city.
I feel the strength of eternal promises murmuring
from the metal of the skyscrapers.
My feet crush these gone lovers' memories
and the night lights me up on fire like a flare gun shot
straight up into the sky.
A picture of hope
the sky made to look like embers
stretching between our hands
locked between a promise and a worry
with birds flying high up above them.
God asked me where I draw my strength from
I told her from the flowers growing inside my veins
that whisper love songs to the night.

Only you know what breaks me down so well.
I wish you could feel the words you say,
The kind of mood you wear for a day.
Do my teardrops settle the storm inside your chest?
If "I love you" were a promise would you keep it just to hurt me?
Was I made from a broken moon?
I don't love you like I used to,
I grew out of the mold we moved into
And bathed in a kerosene light
Screaming, "thank god, thank god. I can fight."

High up on the 7th floor,
you asked me if it hurt
I lied because I wanted it so bad.
The push, the grind, a chance to give birth
to myself with hips that bend without fear.
High up on the 7th floor,
you asked me what was mine
and the glass of the lens of the projector cracked
bending the light in a way that created a
rainbow across my body.

I looked back at you
and you knew.

where you call me

In my head, I can see the most beautiful things. They would never happen, so I started believing that if I could see it, if I could want it enough to dream it, that it wouldn't happen. It couldn't happen.

In my head, I see my older brother and I drinking at a bar & getting along. I'm telling him all of my secrets and all of the men who broke my heart. He's cheering because he knows I deserve better and tells me I'll be alright. For years I could see it, and every year it never happened. We text each other every few months and we say hi quietly as we walk past each other in our parents' home on our way to our own separate lives.

In my head, I see myself performing the most emotional and beautiful song. My voice is powerful, shimmering, and captivating. I am lucid and commanding the stage like a ship set to sail into the Atlantic. But that doesn't happen. I sing inside my walk in closet and nitpick the sound of my voice coming from the audio recording.

In my head, I see myself making these beautiful pictures and films with the most amazing cinematography. I see myself writing stories that could make the most heartless man feel his chest expand to make room for a heart that just got its name. But that doesn't happen. I write monologues in code and bury it under moving images that don't make sense.

In my head, I see myself living in a studio apartment just 20 minutes away from the city. Decorated in plants and always alive with the company of friends. But that doesn't happen.

But when I hear your voice all of it feels possible.
Every night where you call me to tell me
 I'll be okay I can see it all out in the world.

Happening.
Manifesting.
Becoming.

In all the visions I had I never saw you running
 towards me but still there you are very much real,
very much in front of me,
then you leave.

My brother and I shared drinks at the bar and danced with his friends
who told me how loved and supported I am. I sang in public in the metra
tunnel, heard my voice echoing and felt beautiful for once. I made so
many films and poured out all my emotion and celebrated our stories in
my friend's apartment.

But you're gone.

In my head I saw you fully in love with me. Sleeping together in bed,
waking up in the morning to you dragging me out so I could finish our
chores. It happened for four months and then it stopped. Your fear
stopped us, and you let it.

In my head I see beautiful things,
the most beautiful one is the day where you call me.

I woke up New Year's day feeling hazy, feeling free
I brushed away all the dust and debris
I poured her a little bit of water and sent her home to sleep.

Everything felt surreal, out of a dream, I was walking
in between train carts and empty streets
Somehow you found me, in my long denim jacket
You thought it was funny how I could barely get in your seat,
But that didn't stop you from holding my hand,
leaning in, pushing your lips onto mine,
teaching me how to dance with my tongue,
how to live with my heart.

Did my face look like I had fallen in love?
Did it give me away when I said yes to you every day?
We made love in the car he bought for you,
and we made love in a borrowed bed
I didn't care because I was with you,
I didn't care because I knew you'd leave me soon.

Everything felt surreal, out of a dream, I was walking
in between train carts and empty streets
and somehow you found me, spinning tricks like I was winning the
lottery
You thought I was beautiful in red traffic lights,
I think god was warning you to stop
but you kept chasing me, stitching your heartline to mine.

Warning signs, warning signs, warning signs,
I posted them all across your body
telling you I was ready for love, ready for life,
ready for an eternity in the sun and you didn't run.
You stayed in your borrowed bed,
watched me battle ghosts in my sleep,
woke me up with a smile, a pun, and a hug
and for the first time in years I felt safe in January.

paint with my grays and blacks
like you would my yellows and greens.
pour over me a blanket of truths,
paint me a more bearable face
with the colors from my veins;
pulsating my blues with your reds.
take the purples from the 8 o'clock sky
melt them on my back so that I might know
what it's like to fly.
wake me up with the tangerines of your voice,
whispering baby blues and pinks about
how one day I will change.
put your body on my body,
I'll write songs along your spine.
let me leave my mind in the air tonight.
signal flare, take me there
should you want my love
know that I die every night
when your lips dance with mine.
you're a color that doesn't exist.
you're every color I want to wear on my skin.

Fold into the earth and come back
Halved in half and ready to
Be he, who I, who we
Fold back into ourselves
And reach out our hands
For the other our mothers
Taught us not to hold.

We blame you sun, for the fire in men
That scorch our women's bodies and
We blame the sun, that our sons aren't
More honest, more gentle-men.

Boy oh boy, my beds have been made
In the sea, in the mountains where
God came to me and said, my love
Stop pressing the blade against your throat
Grow up and accept that I love you I love you
I love you, I love you!

Fold back into your mother's lap and come back
To me sane and whole to be
He, who, I, who, they
Unfold out to each other
Our mothers begged us to hold.

Every morning I see myself dying and I smile
because there's still enough fight left inside the
quiet corners of my body.
They come out at night after a kissing spree
with the liquor cabinets and they scream
at nightclub lights and preach in baritone cries at church.
I want to be alive, I'm just tired of carrying the moon on my back.

Every night we stayed up
Kissing each other with playlists
Running through the aisles at Walmart
After you pick me up from the metra
Renting our favorite movies from Family Video
My Eternal and your Moonrise
Said I made you feel everything, differently
I cried because my PTSD was louder
Than when you said you loved me
Like the heated lamps on the CTA
You gifted me your warmth
Sheltered me with a nervous affection
You said my tears taste
like Coke in the summer.
A vacation from the stress
Your favorite voice to hear when you're depressed
I looked at you, love of my life
So afraid to love me
That the bones around your lungs cave in
When you hear my name, but still
You dare to bear that kind of pain
Because you want to love me
You want to love me
You want to

I see myself in an empty dance club
the music comes on like lightning cracks the sky in half
I'm there in the middle swinging side to holy side, immaculate.
I move slow with the bass then the
beat comes in and heaven lights up on fire.
I'm gliding across the floor, my soft spirit
held together by my thick frame
and even thicker thighs, I'm stopped in the middle
& I see every boy you chose over me.
Reigning from Joliet to Mendota, they tag along
and try but can't keep up with me.
I'm dropping heat, slinging sweat,
the colored lights fixate on my skin & im alone again.
Robyn comes on & we harmonize
while I think about you kissing everyone who isn't me
& you thought by now my legs would be tired
but like lightning cracks the sky in half,
my legs tear the dance floor up in thirds.
Over here is the past,
here is the present,
and over there is the future &
I am reigning supreme in all of them,
in love with not only you
but also with the best company
anyone could ever keep.

You are a
War I can't
Win

You are a
War I can't
Lose

You are a
War I don't
Want

You are a
War I couldn't
Fight

You are a
War worth
Dying for

You are a
War I march
Towards

Don't dress me up in apologies,
When the only fabric you're spinning
Comes from the red silk you cut
Off the cloth in your veins.

My naked friend lays in his bed performing
a role you helped me write for him.
you saw the edges of my face
twist and shape into that of a man who would
kiss you at your friend's apartment
fly two thousand miles and cheat on you

We drove to Malibu and on every cliffside
valley I saw your eyes shift and tremble
with jealousy that did not belong, a distant tone
that I didn't deserve
I chose to smile while I
tried sharing my first time
in my dream state with you
but you saw your ex in me.
In some light you felt the tremors of my voice
bend and echo into that of a man who would
pick up your call, lie to you, and dive into a dust settled
ocean with an unrequited college crush.

I flooded your room with honesty
a declaration of truth that halted your past
and gifted you a rarity of chance
a man so in love with you
he wanted to understand

By the time you hung up
It was raining in L.A.

I want to explore haunted mansions and fight off ghosts with you.
Get dressed up, put a smile on, find a table for two
Sing old classics, put on a show with a view.
Just take a moment to look at you
Sweating out your lungs, smiling, as you karaoke dream
Video dance out your love for me.
Make me your violent overnight fuck,
your quiet good morning front.

Wild flowers grow in the space between your arm and mine
In my head I do it all wrong, in my head I just want do you all night long
Something about you and I just makes the night want to cry
And I won't lie baby boy, I could never get you off my mind.

Walk me down through the aisles at the arcade
Pretend you forgot how to hold my hand,
I'll teach you again and again.
I'll find you at a late night diner
making wishes out of empty milkshakes.
Pull up in the middle of the parking lot
Take me home to your passenger seat.
Remind me why I never chose to leave.

Fight me with a kiss in the arcade light
Plug your heart into mine with the car radio on high
Play that song that always takes me back to you
The one where the guy is drunk and missing his boo.

Steal me away from the moon
She's jealous because I have you.
Kiss me far, kiss me gone.
Block my number, cause the night is still young.

Find me lost inside the games at the arcade
In smash arenas and mario kart maps
You taste like fear, and
god dammit I've never been so afraid

to forget how to hold your hand,
will you teach me again?

You fell in love in a pond
made out of the gutter from this midnight love
And I hear sounds coming from the metra train
in your bedroom alarm
Maybe it was real for me but I'll fake it every day
until this fantasy isn't a reality
born from my heart, stitched to your fault

I see it down every road
In a never-ending summer mood, a timeless honeymoon
Waiting for it, praying for it
I swim in the deep end of silence
And all I hear coming back to me
Is a train cart symphony
Coughing up the bad blood between us.

If I'll find something, maybe I'll find nothing
Only losers rush to the taste and all I'm good at is losing
And with you I might as well have lost all my weight
Because my feet just can't reach the ground.

I know you're feeling it too
This hurricane heat, this tropical flow
When I outgrew you, it didn't show
Cause I'm still in love with the fevered sweat
made out of the Sunday mornings we kept.

You poured your hard feelings all over me,
Took out your emotion and painted it on top of me
turned me into an ocean with all the blues you stole from the sky
But the joke's on me, I'm out here on a limb
And you're terrified to swim.

Who am I loyal to
When I'm loyal to the sun my body burns
When I'm loyal to the moon my body floods.
I thought it would be better if I were more loyal to human bodies.
When I'm loyal to men I'm raped
When I'm loyal to women I'm betrayed.

Am I too grown for games,
Am I too young to know better,
Who am I loyal to when I'm loyal to you
I'm lit up so bright I trip over my words
And the shape of the smoke your body leaves behind
Is more beautiful than you could ever be.

Who am I loyal to
When I'm loyal to the dusk my lungs drop beneath their weight
When I'm loyal to dawn my eyes dry out.
I thought it would be better
If I let you touch me
But my chest is overflowing
And you've always wanted to see the ocean.

I eat daisies to fill my stomach with beauty and life.
Sucking on their paper taste reminds me of how my hips
command the dance floor.
Left and right, the sensation of being
admired because here is
a thick boy directing his body weight sensually
in a way that makes
his sweat fall like rain on a Saturday
when you're on your way to the market
to grab some smokes and a snack to enjoy
walking in the wet amen of the sky
while listening to your sadboi playlists.
Here he is, in his prime celebrating himself
despite how ridiculous he might look
and he is me.

I'm glued to the fever of the night
and I'm stuck on this tension you built between us.
I'm catching feelings in bed, spitting them back onto the floor.
Baby boy, I let my feelings fall out of me like a tulle skirt waterfall
cascading with my trauma and my goddamn melodrama.
You can't have the prettiest parts of me without the ugliest,
my heaven without my hell.

imagine:
you get in your car, you call him up.
he gets in your car with blankets, a laptop,
and a couple of snacks.
You hug, you kiss, it's been so long but still it
feels like yesterday you sang with each other
in a big empty karaoke room.
He shows you just where to drive and
you stop at his favorite field.
You both jump in the backseat,
laptop perched right in the middle of the front two seats,
blanket stretched between your bodies.
You hold him and his weight greets your chest
with a warm familiar verve that moves you to tears.
He somehow feels it and turns to face you
and wipes it clean off your face.
He stares and kisses you one more time
before asking what movie you want to see.
You're holding each other and after a while
you start to ask him why this spot, why this field?
 He pauses the movie, tells you to put on your coat
and gets out of the car.
The sun starts kissing the horizon
and he takes your hand and leads you closer out
into the field where there is an old construction site left unfinished.

He looks at you and tells you:

"I wanted our first moments being back together to be right where I mourned losing you the first time. Here was where a dear friend drove me so I could make that one image for my book of me standing tall praying to heaven for the strength to continue moving through the world without you. I believe in love, I believe in hope, and I believe everything happens for a reason. I don't know if you and I are meant to be together forever but I do know I love you enough to write a thousand stories and poems about us, enough to make images about us, enough to admit to the world that I am soft for you. And for now, only you. I can't predict the future, I can only promise what I can deliver. And I know for a fact that I can deliver on always putting my best foot forward and ensuring I start and end my days letting you know I love you and want you to be happy."

The sun starts to color the sky
and he walks closer to you.
You can't stop staring in his eyes
and you don't know what to say,
you are so overwhelmed all you
 want to do is kiss him.
So the sun rises, your lips meet his,
and a new day begins.
Imagine that.

Do you think flowers will grow here?
Under the rubble of the city we built,
over the temple where you prayed to my body
every morning and every night?
Do you think flowers will grow here?
At the dinner table where you chewed on my love
and left me with dirty plates?
Will gardens bloom in the desert
where I begged for water
and you gave me a drought?
I'm looking back and it's such a wonder
if flowers can grow where the ground is burned.
If they can bloom in spite of the deadly heat,
then so can I.

Yes.

So can I.

I saw myself through the darkest parts of my trauma
until I didn't recognize my face
and I came out of it bathing in the warm light of yours.
I wish for you to heal, for you to find meaning in the
spaces where you couldn't find it.
and I hope you can hang with your bad weather
as beautifully as I can hang with mine.
It's only after a storm that a forest can thrive.

Love is a multicultural language
with so many faces & rituals.
Not everyone loves the same way
and I think that's beautiful.
Love isn't happiness.
It is an action, a choice.
Love isn't attachment
love is looking at your mortality
and saying thank you
for the moments it broke,
bent, and birthed you.
Love is the experience of all emotions
and making the choice to move forward with them.

Love is you talking to your anxiety
when it weighs heavy on your chest and
listening to what it has to say until
it is quiet.

It is the discomfort
before the peace
the smile across your cheek
when your favorite movie is on TV,
it is being able to breathe even
when you're alone out in the street.

Love is you
& it is me.

I hope you & your family find healing
I hope you can confide in your friends
I hope you & your boyfriend can find love
I hope you reach a peace that can set you free.
All these months
All this silence
I've got nothing
But love & hope.
For not only you
but for myself too.

loverboi.

Sometimes I wish I could be different.

Like I could be enough and not too much all at once so that I don't spill when you trip over a bump in the road you filled with gravel and fear. What if I never told you I loved you? if I stayed quiet on the car rides home? If when I got off that train I walked the other way? I don't think any of it matters because when I walk down empty halls and loud avenues I can feel you calling me all anxious to wonder if I'll pick up the phone to listen to you admit that you miss me.

Sometimes I wish things were different. Like we could've figured out the problems before the afternoon hit and the evening came to take me away from you. I don't think I fucked it up. I couldn't have, because I'm radiant, I am light. I forgave and I loved and I stayed.

Even now, months or years later, if you met me down that tunnel I would run to you, but I need to make my peace with the truth.

You're gone and I love you isn't enough.

It's never enough especially when you close yourself off to it.

I'm a liability, a storm, a garden, a hospital, an ocean. A long list of nouns and adjectives that have become synonyms of your favorite things postmarked and listed on the bottom left hand corner of your heart.

I hope one day I get to see how much you've grown. How much you've conquered your fears and said "i love you" to your reflection in the mirror.

For now I'll remodel the room I made for you inside of me.

Take your posters down and keep them tucked behind the desks where I'll write stories about us. I'll fill the empty space with so many plants and so many succulents. It'll be somewhere I can run to when I miss you and open up the box of polaroids. I'll visit you here. I'll put on Elton John's "Bennie + The Jets" and dance mindlessly to the beat until "Tiny Dancer" comes on and my eyes start to swell up because I'll somehow hear you singing it to me again.

The neighbors will watch me, the cinematic overdramatic loverboi, slow dance with my loneliness while the stars above cry happily as they fall down for me.

I am all that is left of us and it is all mine.

The road to my heart is so pretty.
It's a minefield of evergreens ready to blow.
There's a fork in the road: one is a u-turn,
the other is a landfill full of angry rottweilers.
When you walk by them they will bark at every step.
They will growl and they will run to you.
The sun will start to set, the dogs will be closing in,
the road behind you will disappear.
I've lured you into my trap, a place where
all my lovers die from fear.
In the pit where my blood is brewed,
in the spot where my muscle is torn.
What gives you the right to keep walking?
What gives you the strength?
The dogs are closing in:
5, 4, 3, 2, 1.

The road to my heart is so pretty.
It's a desert with an oasis in the middle.
There is a husky drinking from the water.
He walks over to the spot under the tree
and nestles into his homemade bed.
When you walk by him his ears perk up
and he starts panting, eager to see
if you want to play fetch.
The sun will start to rise,
the water will level itself into the perfect temperature
and I will appear floating in the middle.
Laughing, washing my hair.
I'll catch you staring at me with a smile and ask,
"Can you hold your breath with me?"
Time will start to move faster
And you'll have to make a choice:
5, 4, 3, 2, 1.

the road to my heart is so pretty

We met after nine
You parked your car and kept the radio playing
An album from the wedding band right in my driveway
Spelling out an overdue apology.
Your hands were shaking like tectonic plates shifting
"I love you" is too strong a sentence for you
And you were rehearsing just what to say
as you walked up to me
Nervous, scared, and happy
I hugged you and felt your weight
Press against every pressure point on my body
You buried your head into my hair and breathed me in
I felt your smile take shape as you strung out
the first words you said to me,

"You smell just like your house."

I'm cleaning your wounds while
Dressing mine with a million smiles
Red lights, and late nights.
We met after nine
On top of a rooftop
lifting the sun up from its sleep.
Red tangerine, you see me
One last time before you leave.

You are just like my father: the architect.
Designing metal boxes to contain my heart
while you travel the world without me.
You come home, leave your phone on the counter
And look over your shoulder
scared that I figured out
A way to leave your metal box.
Imagine, an earthquake that doesn't move
the tile on your kitchen floor but still moves.
The only thing that tips over
are the scales between you and me.
I am an opera written by my mother
Performed by the dreams you design
In your sleep, you imagine my voice
melting the citadel walls your father built
to keep you from roaming too far.
And like your mother, you still choose to be
the audience member who runs out during intermission.
Because the language I sing
You don't know how to speak.

I take a little breather,
I walk around for a minute or two.
I listen to the sounds my body makes when
it sighs out relief.
Images beam in, beam out.

Blues and reds,
weaving in, weaving out
letters spelling "My everything".
He stole permission, disarmed me
broke into the mold that carries me.
Yelling with his bullhorn
Sweet mediocrities
into the crevices of my mind.
Where no one, not even the clinician
Can take those words and pull them out of me.
With every robbery,
My body starts becoming
Everything and nothing
The clinician snaps my back in half
And then my eyes cut to black.

The clinician wakes me up.
Hands me a glass of water.
I close my eyes, drink the glass empty
Filling the hell inside me with a 15 minute break.
I step outside, walk around the block and realize it's summer.
A bee flies near me while I wait for my mother.
It lands on my right arm as it mistakes me for a flower
And dies when it stings me.

Teach me how to give birth
without tearing my own flesh.
My spirit is endless, my body is not.
You are marching a summer heat
into my winter bones.

"I am not ready to receive you",
said my heart to the blood in my veins.
"I am not ready to leave you."

If I could construct my universe
I would use your hips as the mold
and your lips as the sun.

fuck me in my childhood bedroom.
while you're sucking on my thighs
the projector streams every memory he ripped out of me,
held up to the sun and made new again.
your tongue will taste like his,
your dick will feel foreign,
but I'm great at translating.
stop talking and let me imagine
that he's inside me,
worshipping every roll,
every part of my skin
he told me he missed.
when we're done you'll want to stay
but when you turn around to give me a kiss
you'll find yourself swept away
into the machine playing dreams.
you were never alive,
you were never fucking me,
you were just another boy I built
to help myself move on from
 someone who lives inside me.

I hold onto hope cause it's all that I have left in me,
I've given all I can I won't take anything from you,
or them, or anyone else. I want to give all that I
can and all I have left is this mile of hope, may it
help you to run where I could only walk.

When I am undone,
when my skin sinks back into the water
where my spirit was born,
when I am undressed to bone and dust,
when I become food for the ocean,
will you sing my name in a love song
or will you leave it in the back of your head
hoping you'll forget?

If I could rip the stars out of the sky,
drain the oceans inside my body,
drink the lava from every volcano,
and build a body that's never known
the unwelcome touch of your hands
then maybe I'd have a chance.
A chance of belonging,
of purpose,
of being more
than a vessel for men
to dump their sins.

I bloom in the winter, digging my roots deeper
into the spring so that when you feel next summer's heat
you'll look up to the sky and think of me.
hope is an action and baby lately all I've been
wanting is to put the work in
put it on me, I'll teach you how to make believe
my body is still a paradise, heaven made earth-bound getaway
I'm in love with my mind, my soul, that boy that changed my life
unblock me, take me out at night, maybe I'll let you
win me at the arcade again.

Kiss my spotless mind, won't you?
Forgive me for keeping score
By edging your crimes into my bones.
Come inside the arboretum
they shaped out of my spine.
A new skylight replaced my mind
and lets the atmosphere breathe
somebody else's memories
in and out of me.
The birds come
with their sad love songs
to teach the lilies
how to grow from the
split in my tongue.
A vision of the Red Sea
parted right where you end
and I begin.

In between the arches of my thighs,
the tender concrete vibrato,
god bestowed upon me
the key to heaven.
The sweet honeysuckle,
the meat padded around my bones
whisper and sigh invitation after invitation.
Why do you deny yourself
safe passage into my paradise?
Weary traveler.
Are you not tired of running?
Take a beat, rest your head,
come inside and unload the weight
of your gravity that goes by
a different name.
Bury your hell inside of me,
let my body writhe in your heat,
say yes to the thunder
that makes all others weak.

Humming.
All I hear is a humming
from a man with a rope inside my head.
His humming bends like my back breaks
over the side of the bed.

His humming moves like the sun
drives cross country across my skin.
All I hear is humming and I am running.
Full speed ahead.
Break the window glass cut my face.
Scar on me a new map that points me to the next heading.
Turn my blood into an architect.
All I hear is humming, he is here and I have already left
him hanging on a swing he tied around my brain
with a noose that's been tightened by other men.

I want to run into a bed of flowers
stay wrapped in their stems for hours.
Fall asleep in champagne dreams
Letting the sky kiss me.

I can be the centerpiece at their wedding,
Will even bring their wedding rings, be like
the petals the flower boy drops on the floor.
I can be okay with never being loved
if I get to be the audience of everyone else's love.
I can be that, I can be a rose on a wall.

Last night, he found me
Under the moonlight
resting on top of hope
he held me close,
hell if I didn't know

Drove around country roads
Where a few of my ghosts waved us home
Please don't break for me right now
I'm floating I don't quite know the feel
Of solid ground beneath my feet

He told me I looked beautiful
In the glow of red traffic lights
I smiled but I thought that it
Was god warning him
Not to fall in love with a boy like me
Look me in the eyes, you'll see
a mirror image staring back
Telling you the same thing

There's a whole world
Outside of you
That tastes sweeter
& goes down softer
And I feel the names
Of every man who
Couldn't love me
cum out of my body
But still I'm left
With yours tucked between lungs
Stuck inside my heart.
There's a whole world
Outside of you
That fucks me
Tender, fucks me better
A world I can let in and out
Of my thighs and let it wear
My name like a Gucci necklace
But still I dance in straight bars alone
Learning a different language that
Can help me say I have let you go
But there's a whole world outside of you
That's bright with the sun and with the stars
It is loud and it is sexy and it is raw
You'll never get to know how beautiful, how warm
That world is because
it's inside of me

He told me I
Looked beautiful
In the glow of red
Traffic lights
Tucked into a borrowed bed
He'd lay on me
And sigh a little bit
He climbed so many men
And found peace on top of me
But still that fear kicked in
With the I don't knows
the could have beens
But he still thinks i
Look beautiful
In red traffic lights

Ask anyone else
Do you think he'd find me beautiful
In the light of day?

I want you to tell the city about
 every avenue you fell in love with me in.
I want you to rip the stars right out of the sky
and hang them up on telephone wires that run
between the suburbs and downtown.
I want you to turn every 24 hour diner
into a wedding chapel.
I'll collect all the gasoline I can find
and pour my nightmares on every wall,
floor, kitchen, and counter.
I'll pass you a box of matches
and cheer you on as you light them up.
I'll stand in the aisle and I'll sing
my favorite love song until you run out.
I'll keep singing as my skin is singed from
the flames and my lungs black.
I'm a lightning rod for disaster, a melancholy firework.
The flames are fed, the sun is rising,
the birds have learned my song and are flying.
Will you still be my standing ovation in the morning?
When the worst and best parts of me have fled me
and I am all that is left,
will you still take me to the city just to kiss me
on the sand at Montrose Beach?

Baby if I'm difficult to read
Just listen to the beat
Hope I'm worth the time
Know I got it made like a dream
Swear I'll stay til
The sun turns grey
We'll pick up that morning shine
Gotta make it thru this weather
Promise you we'll be better.
I can turn the light on
Everywhere you think is dark
Never gonna lie, always got you on my mind
for now I'll stay waitin'
Slow dancin' in my kitchen
With my strawberry shake
At 2am.

I stay faded,
overdosing on the questions
I feed my veins.

Drag me to the basement
and let the surface window light
carve out a getaway for my Holy Ghost.

Unzip me, undo me, unrape me.

Drag me by the hips
and move me down beneath the rafters.
Forfeit my body and sink me in the swimming pool
behind your parent's house.
Take out your phone and film me.
I want to swim with imaginary sharks
so I can practice looking death in the eye.
Hold my head underwater,
take away my lungs, cut me.
Fill the pool with the communion of my blood.
Watch how the deep maroon cascades
around my body like a ribbon.
I bleed beauty, I am beauty.

The sun and the moon couldn't compare to you.
Neither has burned me or downed me in the way
you have with loving hands and a fearful heart.
I've come to find within all the cracks in my skin that I
harbor a kindness, an energy, a love stronger than
any trauma or monster could ever take away from me.
Because in loving you I learned I can love just about
anyone all the while loving myself just the same if not more.
The sun and the moon couldn't compare to you
because you are not a dying star or a roaming satellite.
You are a soul full of paintings
looking for the right canvas to make your home.
I hope you find it.

Suburban boy, are you still mad
At the world for not changing for you
Are you still sitting in the rain
Praying for clouds to lift your pain

I hope you find another way
To chase the night and day
Teach me how to bend gravity
I want my mind to be as heavy
As you make it out to be

Remind me, remind me
Where I left my heart last week
Is it swimming in the creek
Or learning how to dance
On two left feet?
Suburban boy, are you still mad
Because change means you could
give me your all and still risk losing me?

Drive me to the movies
Lock me in between
the sound, the image
Fill my cup with the grain
You scraped off the ceiling
Cleaned with bleach
And named modern art.

Tell them the story about us
Where we met at Union station
And you lit a dumpster fire because
I ripped a hole in my jacket
And you wanted to keep me warm
But didn't want to take yours off.

We lived inside widescreens
Building everything
out of stained glass
and Chardonnay

You played me,
I played you
Not a lot to give
Between two spirits stuck
inside technicolor tropes

Slow it down,
just for a minute
Replay that moment in the story
about us
Where you bruised me
and I deepened the wound

We were living inside a movie
Building every scene out of a memory
We shared with other people
Spread out in between the grain
That only looked beautiful because we were in
Technicolor.

I wanna be in the audience
Clapping before it falls apart
Cheering for the one that got away
To come home to your heart.

I'm a heaven built real enough to feel
A heaven you can't pray to,
but a heaven you can open
your heart and mind to
I'm a heavenly kind of lover
you don't have to sit on your knees
and pray to come get away with me.

He said,
                "You're too much,
                 you're a lot to meet,
              you make a mountain move
               just by looking at me."

We both knew I don't dance quietly,
and maybe it's not what he thought it was,
but it meant the world to me.

That night in the hospital room
His eyes were stuck on me.
Brown-eyed boy don't look so blue.

As long as I got you
My body will heal,
my soul will bloom.
just remember I hung the moon.

He said,
                "You're too good for me,
                 You've placed a fire in my soul,
                   but I don't know
             if I'm worth all this weight on your bones."

Boy all it takes is a little bit of faith
and maybe I wasn't looking for love
But I found a reason to live
you handed me a reason to stay.

That night in the hospital room
my eyes were stuck on you.
Brown-eyed boy don't look so blue
as long as I'm here,
I'm gonna take care of you,
a promise I'll keep is
I'll stay true.

Anything I can do
to keep your eyes from
turning blue.

Put on your favorite movie
Who is he?
Disappearing in between the sex scenes,
he looks like a dream,
a heaven handmade to be believed,
sounds like an angel,
and fucks like the ocean bathes the shore.

Baby, tell me please.
Who is he?
Better when you think
it isn't me, it'll make the time go quick
but here you are
alone in bed having a fit.

Fight or flight,
who is he in between the chase scenes?
A hero, a villain.
A lover tossed out too quickly
A dream you named after me
in this movie stream
you built inside your head.

The feelings it brings,
to be promised a kiss
when your mouth stinks like the creek
that spat me out

The feelings that lift me,
when the greenery my blues overwhelmed
massage my feet.
A welcome mat outside sex's door
reading,

                    "you are beautiful,
                and worth more than a dick could ever spit"

Here it is: The breakup.
The splinter that cracks
your body in halves and
each half tries to pull itself
together.

Take it all in.
Walk into the greenhouse where you grew
different kinds of flowers together.
From when you first met, to your first fight
to the flowers he brought you
when you thought you were going to die.
Walk in the greenhouse for a minute or an hour if you want.
Take it all in. Breathe in the oxygen, exhale the ending.
Realize that you have a choice in what happens next.
You can take out the gas container
your father left in your car for emergencies
wet the greenhouse you've built with gasoline
breathe in the odor and assign it your ex-lover's name.

Walk back to the entrance and light a match.
Let it fall from your grip as you utter their name
and watch the garden you nurtured burn.
Maybe for a minute, or an hour if you want.
Take it all in. Breathe in the fumes, exhale the beginning.

Or

You can rearrange the plants in the greenhouse.
Keep the garden growing through and through
until you reach a better truth about the love you built.
Water each plant and succulent with the tears from your
beautiful brown, green, or multi-colored eyes
and let the greenhouse overflow and overgrow
that now you have to move some plants outside.
Line them around the perimeter of your homemade arboretum
until you've cleared a whole new wing for new plants to grow.

Whatever choice you make,
just make sure it's yours.

I woke up at 2 in the morning
with questions pouring out of my veins
looking to make their way out into your world
but I stopped them and told them to go back to sleep.
I searched for you and there you were
in my hands on a digital screen.
I took a look and saw that boy you talked to in May
a familiar fury ran cross country through my veins
and woke my questions back up
with an alarm that cut through the skin on my chest.

I put my phone back down,
focused on the red light bouncing against my ceiling,
and I let every question I had for you seep out of me
down from my eyes, to my pinchable cheeks
to the pillow on my bed supporting me.

He told me I looked beautiful
in the glow of red traffic lights
so when I opened up my eyes again
I found every answer I was looking for
in the red light bouncing against my ceiling.

I write your ugliness into poetry
& it kisses me back with the sharp reality
that with the bad comes the good
but it's been too many months since
I've seen anything come out of you
that doesn't make me blue.
I spin your beauty into photography
& it hugs me back with the soft promise
that as the seasons change our growing pains
are all a part of the process, letting go & moving on
is really just fancy talk for dancing with the world
letting your pain & your joy lead in tandem
because without one there isn't the other.
Baby I've done so much for you.
I've done so much for me too
but I think time called it.
Let's not talk about what was or what could be
just stay here & feel what is because what it is
is learning better so we can be better, do better.
For the families we build, the lovers we'll keep
oh how we'll finally learn that colors are really
just light that learned to love itself enough to bend.

I tried to kiss you
in a new language
I hadn't learned yet.
How can I say I've forgiven
when I'm still afraid?
In that moment I didn't care,
I couldn't give a shit.
I'd give you a thousand kisses
until I mastered every language,
every dialect, and
every way I could shape
my tongue to tell you,

"it's okay, we're going to be okay."

I'm not good at linguistics,
I barely make for a good
bilingual speaker,
and my emotions run wilder
than the wildebeests in South Africa.
But I would make a Rosetta Stone out of my heart
so I could know, so I could learn,
so I could share so many different
lives with you every time our lips met.

Ask me what I would risk
to have you in my arms
so I could teach you the languages
that have written me back into history.
I'd risk anything, everything,
for a moment, for a lifetime, for a night ride with you.
Kissing the distance between us shut,
kissing to make it all better,
until our wounds are shut in
a history book no one
checks out of the library.

You did something I never thought anyone could.
You took the darkest memory of my life,
the source of all my nightmares,
and you put your love in it.
You turned a trigger into a safe house
and now I'm no longer afraid of the January's to come.

The day you left me you handed me the chance
to open every gate I locked inside my body.
I got to decide if I should remain closed.
In the months that I have missed you
I learned how to turn my gardens
into the public's favorite conservatory.
Everyone loved to visit my waterfalls,
to take pictures by the chrysanthemums,
and to visit the desert room in the warmer corners of my mind.
When you came back for a moment you asked me if I still kept
the succulent you gifted me when we first met.
I told you that it didn't survive my anger after we ended
and I could hear you sigh out a little bit of sadness.

I didn't have the heart to tell you before you left that
the succulent you gave me didn't survive
because I was building another wing.
It's a new hall where the flowers savor color,
where the succulents adorn the walls
and the floor is a river tucked behind glass.
I had the waterfalls, the gardens, and the desert.
All that was left were the final touches of my forgiveness.

You might not ever come back to get a chance to take a tour,
but I'll still take the succulent you gave me
and set it alongside the rest.
Because what you gave me
I want to give to the rest of the world.
A light in the dark, a reason to look forward to waking up,
a place to say sorry and find peace.

I'm sorry to my future love
For how skeptic my heart's become
I'm wired to fight or flight even tho
He's gone, he's gone
I find myself alone at home
Drinking wine and counting crows
Wishing I could love better
Wishing I could fight longer

But I'm still here, living for you
I'll stay here, because I like living for you
I like living for me too
So I'm sorry to my future love
That I've got so many red scars
I still got a few band aids in
The first aid kit my mom left me
So hopefully I'll be ready
To let you in, and let him leave.

You held my hand
Said you didn't know
How to let go of it,
How to hold onto me
It seemed so easy
Believing in this dream
Where our love could defeat
The demons at our feet

But you nailed this rose I gave you
Into walls stronger than us
And you did what men know best
You ran away and asked who's next
Why is it so hard to let love in
to see the sky when all you feel is grey?

Like a flower boy I'll walk you down the aisle
I'll hold your hand and lead you on your way
Throw the pieces of your heart up to the world
I'll be the audience who paid to hear you play
Your loverboi, your ingenue, the reason you brave each new day.

Boy don't give up on your soul
Rip your feet into this great unknown
Believe in make believe and
make it so we can't leave
Without a piece of heaven
Wrapped in between the sheets.

You have the most beautiful name
It's like a song and every time I say it
I feel like I'm calling out to the ocean
In my native tongue
Praying for it to wash me clean
sink my sins beneath the deep

In May I will fly to LA
And I will float out in the pacific
Float until the
Clouds roll in
And the rain beats against
The waves that carry me
I'll look up at the sky
Open my mouth
And receive
holy communion
While your song plays
In the back of my head,

"O.....el mar
O.....el mar
Me quiero quedar
ahí en las olas
Del mar
querido mío
Encuéntrame nadando
O.....en el mar
O.....en el mar"

I want to walk on real sand until
my feet meet again with the Atlantic.
The ocean water will be shy because it's been a while
but it won't hesitate to wrap around my toes and my ankles,
welcoming me so lovingly.
I'll keep walking in, nervous but ready,
and I'll tell him all about where I've been
since the last time I saw him.
He will laugh and cry for me but he will still hold me.
Floating together, the Atlantic and I will kiss
in the form of waves crashing my skin.
My legs spinning cute love notes in its depth.
The Atlantic will take a moment before pulling me
under with a wave to tell me he's missed me.
I'll tell him I missed him too
and we'll look up at the sky together.

"Isn't it beautiful?", I ask the Atlantic.

The Atlantic nods with a gentle wave and tough pull.
I'll be mesmerized by the sky and the Atlantic
will ask me to stay this time.

"I have no reason to leave,
so for now you'll have me", I tell the Atlantic.

I dive in, take him all in, and swim
around in him like a mermaid looking for shiny forks.
I'll come back up for air and the Atlantic will stop me.
He'll tell me he doesn't want me to leave again
and I will know he means it this time.
With a gentle wave and a tough pull,
the Atlantic tells me he loves me as
I surrender my body to him lovingly.

all I see are daisies
humming out memories
lo-fi hip hop beats
and top 40 pop single dreams
wired from the tendons in my left arm
to your right.
I'm a physical love letter
penned by the grace of god
she hands me over to you
and tells you,

        "sink yourself into me
          and let these waves bend,
        break, and birth you into who
        you've always wanted to be."

No...into who you've always
needed someone else to be.

I closed my eyes to listen to my intuition
and let him guide me through all this noise
was it in the static that heaven and hell forged
their truce inside my body?
or the radio silence you handed me
that sunk me deep into a sea of understanding?
all around me is a projection of daisies
that really just turned out to be
the polaroids I set on fire of you and me
happy, in love, sleeping inside of a 35mm dream
imagined in an empty screenwriter's stream
of consciousness,
boy how I've been so self-conscious.
I've asked and I've begged you to teach me
how to say goodbye with a twisted knot in my tongue.
how to unlove you,
unmiss you,
unknow you.

The answers came to me in riddles
in intuition, dreams between us,
and phone calls every 4 months when you decided
maybe you could handle the sound of my voice.
Goodbye isn't a word in my vocabulary,
& my love and passion for you
is really a reflection of my love
& passion for myself.
loving you improved me
missing you elevated me
knowing you launched me
into being a better human being.
you took my PTSD and softened him
loved him & threw him back into the Atlantic
so he could learn to swim side by side
with the whales and sharks of the city.
You took a jaded boy and you molded him
broke him, & reassembled him
into a vision of the future you wanted.
But,

I got to decide who
I would become after
you pulled the plug.

And here I am
in all my glory
thick heart pumping
out love letters to
the world in the role
I was born to play of
the
          overdramatic

               cinematic

                    loverboi.

ricardo bouyett is a puerto rican writer & visual artist creating projects that deconstruct toxic masculinity in an effort to inspire reflection, healing, and progress from trauma. He has been making fine art photography since 2012 evolving from a surrealist composite artist into a powerhouse of self-directed films and photo series'. His most recent fine art collection, *Oh, Bouy*, is a fine art photography series that further examines toxic masculinity through the narrative lens of his recovery from sexual trauma. As a rape survivor he strives to create art that inspires healing, hope, and growth for all.

- *about the author*

loverboi. is a collection of poems that illustrate the arduous and uncomfortable process of self-love which requires accountability, honesty, and growth.

loverboi. acknowledges that the most rewarding lessons are those of forgiveness and reconciliation.

- about the book

CPSIA information can be obtained
at www.ICGtesting.com
Printed in the USA
LVHW042005290419
616026LV00001B/26

9 780368 494109